PATTERN-BOOK

Éireann Lorsung was born and grew up in Minneapolis, Minnesota. She works and teaches in a field of images, objects, movement and texts. Her collections include *Music for Landing Planes By*, *Her book,* and *The Century* (Milkweed Editions). She moved to Ireland in 2022 to teach writing at University College Dublin.

Pattern-book
Pattern-book
Pattern-book
Pattern-book
Pattern-book
Pattern-book
Pattern-book
Pattern-book
Pattern-book
Pattern-book
Pattern-book
Pattern-book
Pattern-book

Éireann Lorsung

CARCANET POETRY

First published in Great Britain in 2025 by
Carcanet
Main Library, The University of Manchester
Oxford Road, Manchester, M13 9PP
www.carcanet.co.uk

A CIP catalogue record for this book is
available from the British Library.

ISBN 978 1 80017 485 6

Book design by Andrew Latimer, Carcanet
Typesetting by LiteBook Prepress Services

The publisher acknowledges financial
assistance from Arts Council England.

CONTENTS

SPELLING

DRAWING

SINGING

ELEGIES

for Shana,
my brothers, their families,
Matt, and my mother
in memoriam my father, W. L.

Pattern, like a magnetic field,
is passionate in restraint

Veronica Forrest-Thomson
'Contours—Homage to Cézanne'

PATTERN-BOOK

SPELLING

Weeds triumphant ranged
Strangers strolled and spelled
At the lone orthography
Of the elder dead

(Dickinson)

POSTCARD TO SHANA WITH PHOTO OF WASHINGTON AVENUE BRIDGE (MINNEAPOLIS)

You said, do you ever look down and think
he jumped from this *high*? We were young. We had

poet-fathers to lean on, and real fathers.
We could ask those questions, because they were

just poets, just fathers to us then.
We crossed the Mississippi several

thousand times those years and every time
I would look down, at air and rocks and water, and

there was the poet, falling.
                    January nights, out late, snow blurring

the spherical lamps, or pumping my bicycle's
pedals as fast as they would go across that

bridge in May, stolen peonies tied
to the rack—we both did what we shouldn't,

each in our own way.
                        When you get this note, it will be

the future. Under cheap polyfil comforters
our students will kiss with the ardour

of those who know the world will never end.
Friendship is a kind of time-machine, it turns out:

I remember your arrival from the place called Paradise
and the smell of hot vinyl in your car. Not long

ago. We sat, two decades back, in my red room
to write the first things we would ever teach.

We flew from that bridge after
the poets we loved. But see. We lived to tell.

SIMILE

How does a simile work?
—Place something next to something
and say, *here*. (The *here* is where
the somethings touch.) The rainy
night, like Debussy.
There on the shelf, a piece

of grapevine in a blue
vase. The world is so much
like itself it can be hard to see.
Tomorrow I will try again
to understand: what is a simile?
All night, all day: the rain

comes in vertical lines,
then horizontal lines,
like a drawing made
on the world I can perceive.
How does the simile do
whatever it is it does to us?

The world is touching
the world itself and touching
me. My hand, this pencil
making all these marks.
A drawing of the world
that is the world, that I
can make. That's making me.

SONNET FOR ORDINARY TIME

A little wind. A little bit of rain.
The first leaves drifting down from ash and oak.
The cosmos, wild now and full of blooms;
the purple furze on bolted artichoke.
Nasturtiums pile. The finches come to land
on sunflowers' heads, that hang toward the ground.
The plums are gone, the apples, too; the corn
stands stripped of every ear, dried out and brown.
Fall's sentence here is clipped—no lengthy phrase
compounding thought and image to express
what's clear for anyone to see. Short days.
Damp air. The blackcap (once again) has left her nest.
The things I struggle for with pen and ear
return in autumn's grammar every year.

WRAPPERS

You may remember all the times they took us to the Russian grocery store
and let us buy chocolates, because I saved (yes, these too)

the wrappers from the candies, printed with nesting dolls, alphabets
I didn't understand. And I can show them to you,

having kept them in this notebook since childhood, and remember
the days we spent in the fabric store next door

among discount bolts of mill-end fabric, bins of buttons as tall
as we were, then. Every time we wanted more buttons, more

candies wrapped in foil or with pictures of ladies in fancy clothes.
We saved them all up. They were beautiful. Worth keeping.

I thought we were rich. We were just barely breaking even.

SECOND BORN

A ring of wool.
A ring of glass.
A ring of iron filings.

A ring of feathers.
My brother's breath becomes
balloons and vases.

A ring of wool
on carding combs,
a ring of filaments of glass.

After dark, some little
sparks still cling
to anvil's underside.

A ring of salt. A ring of ash.
What he gave me, I will keep:
a ring of glass, a ring of wool.

THREE AND FOUR SWANS

For brothers, goose-quills
sewn into wings
with linen thread

and gut-cord,
steel needle, bone
needle. For, brothers,

we'll have winglight,
air thrown by muscle,
streetlamp counter flight.

Not wild, swans
made by hand:
cloth harnesses, leather

crownpieces, cutwork, red
filling stitch not
blood but silk.

Do you like
our bird suits,
brothers? At night

your eyes will shine
in prairie cities,
far from me.

We will break
through fences, we
will launch ourselves

onto wind, sing
with human voices migration
songs over ocean,

over island, over
railway, over airport:
diaspora song, change

song, song of leaving—
songs that mean
no turning now,
no going back.

THE KINGDOM OF CHILDHOOD

The power was out when we woke up.
This was before I had begun to bite my nails,
before our middle brother's glasses, in the room
the colour of a robin's egg. There was a radiator,

a window cloaked in yellow cloth, our red
and yellow and blue plastic cups on the sill.
And our father came in to find us every
morning, carrying the baby in his arms and

a song from the other side of the house:
girls in the woods, whalers in ships,
a man in love on an unfamiliar street,
a house built half on desert, half in forest.

Don't you believe what your parents
sing to you in the dark? Don't you believe
the rain on the window is a code that says
everyone will be safe, forever, and beloved?

When the lights went out in summer
there were white candles in the darkness.
Our father had a bristly beard.
Our mother helped us set the table

while he played the guitar. They were always
singing us to sleep, sewing machine humming
in the next room, and we could believe,
without having to believe, in what dew on grass

and frost on grass in the morning say: again. Again.
The sugar maple giving itself to the fire.
The midnight picnics of Ritz crackers and raisins.
Our father loving our mother all the livelong day.

NEIGHBOURHOOD SPELLS

Through time came the sound of their voices.
When I was born I fell from broken
edges of sidewalks into tunnels made by animals
I never saw. In that other world I had waited for form.

My mother asked six questions, like *who knows*
the name of every plant sprouting from concrete?
Which is the bird who speaks with human words?
Where on the body of the maple do we set

the taps? She built a yellow house inside a brown house
and a red house inside the yellow one. She planted
apples that grafted themselves and multiplied.
From the pink rose came the white flower, from

the white flower came the golden heart. In the box
elder tree a child was calling, opening windows
made of paper and wax. People would touch
my mother on the street with warnings: *don't catch*

your only daughter on fire. Avoid the headwater
of our beloved river until the twenty-eighth month. A girl
you show a bridge is bound to leave. How best
to trap a moth, if not by light? I waited,

fingers crossed, on the other side. Rooms and
rooms of roses, rooms of yellow curtains and wax
paper. Someone began a clapping game. Birth
an exit to crowds of flowers with long thorns.

BRAMBLE CUTTING

Five-petaled, milk-white—say
thin as milk, as wholesome:

pithy centres turn to pulp
in July. All year, canes

overrun garden paths, empty
lots. Bramble is a lesson

in plant economy.
        —In another life

I could be bramble: or
rain on bus shelter roofs,

the taste of salt stepping
off a train. An estuary

in the morning under fog
not to be seen through.

Bunkers overgrown with thicket.
These last times I was a girl.

LINNAEAN SYSTEM

for Nuala

You know the rose is in five pieces.
You know the centre of the split apple copies it.
The skin of a nectarine, a pear, an almond, a peach makes my mouth burn.

My mother's sister is me in a photograph.
Among roses in the wallpaper, on stiff upholstery: two girls.
Almost fifty years ago I see myself sitting in a house I hardly remember.

Family resemblance shows in what my skin reacts to.
You know I can't decide: is the *me* I am my mother or my aunt?
Count the apple, plum, peach, pear, blackberry, cherry, strawberry, rose.

In this large family with its one central name.
In the May evening apple blossoms spread their scent.
Roses copy themselves every summer, all up and down the walls.

The four hands of the two little girls I could be.
Freak mutation of a blue eye, petal sport, widow's peak, helix after helix.
Through the window, the rosebush: yellow flowers timelapse into fruit.

ROSE COUNTRY INVENTORY

A sugar company establishes a woman:
all this up to the edge of an encroaching sea.
Above us in the future, she has another pint
and goes to mow the bowls ground.
Between the chimney pots of terraced houses

blue sky blooms, for just an hour.
Each small town in England stands erect,
five-petaled wild rose goes through.
Fragrant flowers, impassable briar
full of empty packets. Lucozade bottles.

Geese in the public park.
Her face is pink, that woman. Between
houses little wastelands blow.
Mahonia, with its tiny berries,
makes plans to occupy

museums, build a new super-superstore
out of brick leftover from the Blitz.
Rosebushes bloom from June to December:
she stands for nothing but herself.
Someone in hazmat gear has combed

the elementary school, searching for a bomb.
The woman stands by the sea, by the roses.
Town councils decide to fence their parks.
Vomiting at six p.m. is done by anyone,
vomiting at six p.m. on the street outside a pub.

MINNEAPOLIS, EARLY SPRING

At this time of year in this town
the sky is full of boats and branches,
wreathes of fishing line, light
and water tied into bouquets,

and on tall bicycles the crust
punks go riding into pink
twilight as Nina Simone's cover
of 'Suzanne' stops time in one

speaker and gives me an entirely
new way of reading
the crumbs on the tablecloth,
the movement of constellations

as hands and pianos and headphones,
and the dark blue sheet with stars
in it that means *forsythia in March.*
Go walk. City streets

overarched by apple blossom make
their own covenants and the river
is full of stars under the collapsing
bridge. Condition of possibility,

your name is *Minneapolis*, a name
that came much later than the land
and means: *took this.* And put fixed
wooden houses. Thing called

the past floats just under the top
layer of water, catching facts
of time and place in it, catching
me and my bicycle and the crustpunks

and the food co-ops and the theatre
students rushing into the Brutalist
building in their leotards, holding
up the planets and the moon.

With lilacs, with daffodils
and tulips stolen from university
beds, with the invention
of the front yard, the lawn

mower, paper routes, radio
programming, peonies relaxing
onto the sward outside Richardsonian
Romanesque classroom buildings.

Snow's going sends rot into the air.
Let us all spring praise the express
bus running overnight with windows
ablaze! We walk bridges, sing

the last ice melting. We interpret
the boats below us as islands.
We wear secondhand everything
from the thrift-shop's dollar counters.

We hold out a broken apple branch
as if it is a torch. By a willow fence
a dog exclaims: *Here!* We are.
Down Lake Street, orange lamps,

the library opens its arms.
Women walk into the last blizzard
searching for tent-sleepers, passing
out handwarmer packets. Lyme

creeps northward on the bodies
of brown mice. Nothing resolves.
The world stays multiplied in the river.
Spring arrives, secretly, all one night,

holding a mirror, like a tide
full of boats no one thought
would return, like a young person
ready to be everyone's lover.

VOCATIONAL EDUCATION

for Ray González and Michael Dennis Browne

I sure *do* want to live in a world where poets
teaching at land-grant universities in the middle
of prairies, in May, through those big old wood-
mullioned windows, see that *finally* the cherry
trees have begun not only to bud but to bloom; a world
in which such poets, paying no mind to two
hundred gawking undergraduates, simply raise
the sashes of those dark-wood windows, step
high over the ground-floor sills, and lower themselves
out onto the plush grass to walk—or maybe in workshop
the word we'd fight for would be *saunter*—through that grass,
the *handkerchief*, the *remembrancer designedly dropt* of it,
all the way to where the trees are losing their very first
petals; a world in which those poets stand there, under
the cherry trees, their serious shoes somehow lost
on the way, barefoot now, in the middle of the beginning
of the Midwestern spring, while buses accelerate
over bridges and bulb flowers stick their slender fingers
out of the rich earth and the gaping windows
of the university frame two hundred of us who,
hmmm, someday, yes, would like to dare to do that too.

SONNET FOR THE SECOND-LANGUAGE SPEAKER

What is a word? — Depends on who you ask.
For instance, in the rigid Flemish taal,
so many things that feel like words don't pass,
and my sprung language doesn't work at all.
My sentences are yet another place
where stringent rule-embracers don't agree:
to me, an error shows the second face
of grammar. The mistakes *are* what I mean.
The thing I value most in any line—
drawn, made, wrote, thought; in fantasy or fact—
is flexibility: that, like a spine,
the art supports the mind by which it's maked.
What use is language flattened, dried in books?
Our language lives most when it is mistook.

SONNET FOR THE PHILOSOPHY OF LANGUAGE

Is there a world outside of metaphor?
Is there a *something-there* beyond the words
I use to name the things I know that are?
Is there a way to touch the *is* that is 'the bird'?
How does it come to be that unlike things,
when in a double figure, actually
suggest that (e.g.) church bells, as they ring,
are everything they *are* by language we
employ? When Hopkins' kestrel hovers in
the air, is it a bird or is it deity?
Is what it *means* in fact the space between
these words that only meet imperfectly?
—Is 'world' *in* language? Does 'meaning' inhere
at points where image mutually appears?

DRAWING

FEBRUARY MOTHER

i.m. E.M.

There is no way to do in language what is done in paint.
No way to do in paint what language does. Both

so frail in the face of the world's transient *everything*.
The year passes by, the years pass, snow comes again.

Under haystacks mice find shelter; in the dooryard
of the white house pigeons eat scattered grain. A star rises.

I pass through the ultramarine of the tympanum into dun
February, find you warming your legs by a fourteenth-

century fire, your blue dress above your knees as the water
bearer pours without end their beaker into a sky

two fish swim through. Here below, the world is lead white
and a whiter disc ascends its winter sky. You are leading

your donkey up a hill now, laden with kindling. The house-shaped
haystacks under caps of snow are gold, but the ash

trees and oak trees, your wimple, your kirtle, your hood, the distant
smoke itself are all the colour of smoke. You throw down seed

for grey birds, their black-banded wings at your feet
for kernels of corn. There is blue everywhere in painting.

—What's the point of it?
                                        This morning your sister
became the water poured from the mouth of the sky and

the scales growing in all perfection from the body of the fish,
the magpies' feathers and the mist. What's the point of this world

such blue moves through without miracles, our ordinary
world and its ordinary time? Nothing holds still and yet

I have a sense of history as if it were a picture: *here* the donkey
struggles uphill under its load of sticks, and *here* the pigeons

pick at grain. The fire never burns out. No one dies. The world
is always there, under the tympanum's perfect sky. The point

of the painted world is the blue of our world that lives
and dies. There is no other point but that.

BROKEN BLUE AND WHITE HANDLED MUG, MAKER UNIDENTIFIED

Portland Museum of Art (Maine, US)
Collection number P845

In the foreground on broken ceramic, life
continues. Nothing is stopping the horseman

from lifting his whip, the cows from cudding,
the clouds from lifting into atmospheric

shade; nothing keeps the trees' shadows from
producing their own ongoing depth. The band

of open flat-faced five-petaled roses I can *almost*
see as pink proceeds as always, one inch high,

around the rim. But brokenness is permanent: the hand
that guided transfer onto bisque has stilled.

And though my own hand, sympathetic to the broken
cup, might reach to hold it or perceive the weight

of a like vessel I once held, it will *not* hold; half
the mug is gone.

                                        There is no way
to join *now* to the past, hidden perfect in memory as if

in some museum's forgotten drawers. Like a dream
I only partway can recall, the broken edge reveals

the paste but not the workshop bench, not the hands
that ably laid the transfer on the bisque from day to day.

Trees climb the hill under a Staffordshire sky. The man
driving the horse drives it on. Under clay in marked

or unmarked plots lie hands that guided roses
around the edge of ordinary cups. In the blue

of this unchanging *now*, swallows permanently
swoop, singing a long-gone summer in—

as if one day they'll find the missing piece of sky,
that missing piece which, more than all that *is*, is there.

THE MOON OVER MAGRITTE'S LANDSCAPE

In the low lands near the Leie it is early evening,
and the sky is the blue of sonnets and summers'

days, but the moon is Belgian and is yours, painter:
dangling by a thread from an astronaut's unimaginable

finger, way out beyond our reckoning. I'm here
on earth with you, in the nacre of nightfall

where the pig farmer next door slides the barn open
and the draft horse charges out into humidity

stirring up stars of dust with her hooves, her milk-
pale foal following her under the arch of roses

that open all at once, like the mouths of children
at the movies seeing the screen come alive for the first

time. The hands of the clock wind forward exclusively.
No one waits for us, not in the yellow stone

hallway of the central station, not at the umbrella
seller's shop. So we'll go together, out along the canal

as always, on our bicycles, racing the draft horse
the length of her paddock, racing the clock as it numbers

minutes faster than we can count, summers
on springs, winters on autumns, apples rolling

from where they are piled in orchards, as workers
move among the pruned trees taking those green

apples that float in our dreams, that are carried
in crates downriver toward the North Sea. Has

evening left us? Has morning come already? We will
walk right to the edge of it together. Hold

my hand: like this, I can reach into the tree of day
and lift back to you two perfect fruits. The space

station reduces to a speck. The migrating pickers gather
in their red smocks, a line I like better than a border.

In the distance, trains go back and forth, carrying
their loads of movie stars and rocket fuel, national

anthems, schools of painting, trade agreements. All
together now: and waves go back and forth from England

to here. Could we have seen the future from out in space?
No? Well I think we got what we came for anyway,

Magritte: the lamp turns on next to the door. On Earth
it's evening now. The sky is light. The sky is light.

POSTCARD TO SHANA WITH PHOTOGRAPH OF FLORALIËN GHENT, 1913

Everyone I know is losing cities this year. Yesterday
I heard the cuckoo for the first time, which means

it's spring. Since I last wrote, teams of gardeners
have gone to work all over Ghent, secateurs catching

light; in days the neighbourhood was transformed.
Gardenias, azaleas. A young man stood near a shallow

pool breaking flowers from a peach branch and setting
them in water. Industry unrecognizable in its new

horticultural clothes. You know I have been tending
to an orchard of my own: peach tree and cherry

trees; apples; plum. The lawn is stippled bright with daffodils.
I thought, *if I leave him I will lose the garden*

I made. I thought, *I can make another garden anytime.*
Nevertheless (the lambs are playing now—again!), I stayed.

THE GARDEN AT THE EDGE OF THE WORLD

Perfume of apples in September: warm
and sweet-sour. High hay,

all day under arches of sky, lindens long
past their sweetness.

We left tall lilies among the stink
of box hedges. Left roses

and columbine, quince, strawberries'
second cropping hanging

from wood boxes. Sheep in
their pen ran to us, passing.

Have been lying among tall
grasses, in linen so fine a hand

shows behind it. Lying among
rivers that thread their way through us.

Chamomile white against
gathering dimness. Still here, where

corn crake and cuckoo
sound a last sonnet. Under sky-arch

and apples, tall grasses like
water, sharpness of autumn, blue everywhere.

DESIDERATA

reverie alone will do (Dickinson)

Tall, thin-stemmed buttercups, green queen-anne's-lace
across and over stems of taller grass, dark
stripe of a walnut, an ash.
Walking the meadow, there is little
to want but walking, and
a meadow. Pigeons' shadows
settling in new rows of cabbage
one field on. Now clouds pass
the sun, for a moment, and are gone,
and everything retains
its gold, and all
we need is in this
meadow, its
umbels and its star-
shaped yellow heads of ragwort
and, floating off somewhere,
a train's sound.
Then gone. Then the quiet of the meadow,
which is not quiet if we
listen to it: but is ticking,
buzzing; whirr of wingcase
(a red insect rises) and trill
of a pipit, airgun's pop, our
voices, low—all the future and the past
in them, in the meadow, without end, without any end—

A NOTE ON EARLY FLEMISH PAINTING

after the Ghent Altarpiece, also called
The Adoration of the Mystic Lamb

In disregarded foreground (underneath
patrons, awestruck, at each panel's edge),
out of sight of God's eye, which rolls up
the azure gradient of a flattened sky,
careful studies of the unessential
take their place: dill, borage, common daisy,
mint; mallow, tansy, comfrey, dandelion—
Van Eyck's hand was restless, the flowers say,

and so he painted us, *who toil not*
(and neither do we spin). Some people claim
the painting's work is evangel: the dove,
the hand, the wheel; baptizer, maid, and monk.
Central among rays and lilies, by the lamb
the chosen people kneel. —But we're *the field.*

WATERWAY CONNECTING THE CITY TO THE SEA: IMAGE AND COMMENTARY

after the Ghent Altarpiece, also called
The Adoration of the Mystic Lamb

Contrary
to popular
opinion
it exists
for reasons
other than
to home
the weird
dog-faced
dolphins
left after
the end
of the late
middle ages.

Also to support the production
of flax, which must rot
in it, and pomegranates,
which bristle on improbable
trees above it, and citrus,
and olive groves; and to locate
a flight of birds heading out
of the picture in a V-formation;
and to embrace the humid bodies
of female hermits;
and to reflect the sky;
and to subside into the ground;
and to return in the spring,
with the thaw, the very image of mercy.

SIGNIFICATION

after the Ghent Altarpiece, also called
The Adoration of the Mystic Lamb

Let *angel* mean *musician*. Momentar-
ily. Let *painter* mean *the figures on*
flat ground. Let *Adam* mean the *tuft* in *tuft-*
ed vetch. Let *borage* stand for *city on*

a hill. Let *Hubert* bear the letter *young-*
er bro. Let *personage* bring *ma-*
sterpiece to bear. *Geography* the *on-*
of *onlooker*. Let *earth* take on

the meaning *sacrifice*. Let *Gentiles* sig-
nify *The Mystic Lamb*. *Inspiration*
mean only *breath comes in*. Let *testimon-*
y mean that *I was There*. Let *hand* mean *enter*

side, and *man*, and *doubt*. *Colour* only *light*.
Let *painting*, in the end, mean just *Amen*.

PAINTING IN NINE PARTS

for M.P.

The first part is the onset of summer, finally, on a July day after weeks of grey. There was no warning. The river was high and brown from late long rains.

The second part is purple lupines.

The third part is a yellow gravel path or a scrambling path up rocks.

The fourth part is dingy upholstery, waxy where many hands have rubbed, and the sound of glassware being taken away, and carpet patterned with scrolls, and rain spattering on the glass, and a fire in the fireplace, and the pleasant noise of others' conversation.

The fifth part is desire; but every part is desire.

The sixth part is a west-facing window and a lack of curtains or an unwillingness to close them, so that once the light has gone the person is visible through the window, standing at the table.

The seventh part of painting is painting itself.

The eighth part is gravity, or perhaps the word is graveness: a silence that hangs around certain human beings.

The ninth part is bathing in that river, after the rains have gone, sitting alongside that river on the first hot afternoon; the ninth part is the arrangement of painters on a rock across the narrows; it is a certain back, bent under a beach umbrella; the ninth part of painting is writing in invisible letters the name of the place to which you will not return.

CORONA BOREALIS

Shore of Lake Superior studded with provincial parks and at eight
p.m. smell of a human's an animal smell rising from a skin of water
I never touched/I went through insensibly leaving teeth on cobbled

shore I wouldn't see again for years meanwhile no salt lifted from water
and no boys disappeared among birches to unbecome eight years old
to wade backward through childhood invisible-untouchable by threats

named northern Minnesota/northwestern Ontario, two-room huts
under immense blue/blue-going-dark as easterly chains of bright water
form martens infinitely chasing inverse bows across these young eight

counties (Cook/Lake/St Louis/Koochiching/Itasca/Carlton/Pine/
Aitkin) across disappearances in progress here (language variants: eight
ore ships: twelve) but rising (yes) still rising to shine double in water

SONNET WITH A QUOTATION FROM MILLAY

If I should learn, in some quite casual way
the facts of how you wed, and who, and where,
and if I came upon (on Facebook, say)
her dress or your engagement photos there,
I would return to nights we spent as kids—
when we thought we were grown (though we were not)—
in ill-lit rooms, as outside katydids
eclipsed our whispers, and we nodded off.

I'm not your wife. I might have been, but: no.
And yet I keep returning to the years
when you and I together in the snow
would stamp our names—unlasting souvenirs—
and what we promised then. No marriage vow,
I find myself still faithful to it now.

SINGING

AUTUMN SONG

A hedgerow with a hole in it, a loop of amber.
Beech leaves and (out in the countryside) ripe grain.
Childhood under branches of linden, in fields of chamomile.
Everything between the summer and the autumn indicated days of rain,
weeks of rain, the river filling to its banks and overtopping.
Hazel edged with frost, bramble tipped with frost.
In the small fields between a stream and an ochre river, a hedgerow
with a hole in it.
Looping a hundred feet high a dozen swallows, a fieldfare.
Now there is no way to be near the river without nitrogen, phosphates.
Redoubling cells in the body of the red-winged thrush, the fieldfare.
Some repetition is seemly: red-winged thrushes, a dozen swallows.
The daily work of shopping and cooking and driving and bickering.
Wanted the poem to be a hole in a hedgerow.

A tractor made loops in fields of ochre, and a river.
Beech leaves and bus stops, hawthorn berries, bramble.
Daylight over an amber field, over an ochre river, a dozen swallows.
Everything between the summer and the autumn was chamomile
and poppies in the verges.
Fluorescent lights in train stations overnight, and hawthorn berries, and
hazel edged with frost.
Grain ripening, the river overtopping, the fieldfare just beyond the field
of bramble.
In the small fields between hedgerows a tractor applying manure.
In the small fields of the breath and the voice.
My childhood transplanted 6,000 miles, a lake in summer surrounded
by catkins.
Outside, a holy field, a fieldfare looping above a nitrogen river.
Rain in the distance above a holy field, a tractor.
The row of arbor vitae along tracks: a train stops for suicides.

Through the hole in the hedgerow watch the last of the grain brought in
by red harvesters.
Under sleeping bags and in train stations and collapsing in doorways.

A tractor made loops in fields of ochre.
Bramble jam, a loss in a landscape endlessly old.
Childhood looping like a high school filmstrip of cells redoubling.
Dozens of swallows over grain ripening, the flax harvest
brought in months ago.
Everything between the summer and the autumn was wild roses
in hedgerows.
Fluorescent lights in train stations overnight, but just beyond
the darkness a field of bramble and willows.
Grain ripening and fluorescent lights in train stations, bus stops.
Hawthorn berries against a textile scrim of copper leaves—hay in, field
empty, willow yellow haze to mark the end of ochre.
I forgot the voice and breath themselves may be witness and resistance.
In hedgerows rabbits hiding, voles hiding; in ochre hedgerows,
in red-tipped hedgerows.
In holy fields the remainder of phosphates.
In the small fields between hedgerows a tractor looping and looping.
Losing nitrogen from manure applied in winter to the river.
My train stations transplanted 6,000 miles, fluorescence shining in a
summer night.
Nitrogen overtopping the river in summer rain.
Out in the city and in the countryside, the daily work of cooking, eating,
bickering, sleeping.
Rain piercing multiply an ochre river.
Some unseen worry at a stone margin.
The fieldfare, the red-winged thrush, the tractor, the summer rain.
Under five-fingered chestnut leaves going gold in a furze of rotting buxus.
Wanted the poem to be a place of singing.

A tractor making a river in amber or in ochre.
A tractor making loops; fields, an ochre river.
By bramble, by candlelight, a tractor looping in ochre; a hedgerow.
Fluorescent lights in train stations overnight, and, just beyond the
    fieldfare hunting in a copper field.
Grain ripening and hawthorn berries in a loop of amber.
In the evenings fluorescent lights humming on in train stations.
In the small towns high-water flood marks ochre on white walls.
Nitrogen overtopping the train tracks in summer rain.
Redoubling cells in the bodies of the dozen swallows, the fieldfare.
Then over the hedge the frost-edged leaves of hazel.
While fluorescent lights illuminated train stations in a way I wasn't
    used to.

A yellow haze across the field, across the three-lane highway.
And as amber caught in gutters battered by water.
Childhood along the overtopping river, awoken at midnight
    to bail out the house.
Dying in hospitals and on doorsteps and under a sheet of corrugated card
    on a forced-air grate and collapsing in doorways.
Fluorescent lights in train stations overnight, but just beyond the fieldfare
    hunting in a copper field.
In a loop of amber, a little ring of amber.
My small streams transplanted 6,000 miles, looping and looping.
Nitrogen overtopping the field edge in summer rain.
Out there in the distance, a fieldfare looping above the daily work
    of cooking, sleeping, bickering, walking.
Rain redoubling as cells in the body of the red-winged thrush,
    the fieldfare redouble.
Summer rain and red-winged thrushes, fieldfare in an ochre field.
Then over the hedge the last of the fall raspberries.
Wanted the poem to be the ordinary work of cooking, commuting,
    bickering, thinking.

A tractor: made loops, ochre, fields, a river, a hedgerow with a hole in it.
And as amber coin-shaped leaves accumulated in gutters people went
about the daily work of shopping and cooking and driving and
bickering.
Arbor vitae along train tracks where cars stop for rail crossing arms.
Everything between the summer and the autumn was beeches shading
bus stops.
Fluorescent lights in train stations overnight, but just beyond the fieldfare
hunting in an ochre field.
Grain ripening and hawthorn berries.
In hidden gardens human sorrow drowns itself, under the yellow willow,
under the amber beech.
Losing nitrogen into an ochre river.
Redoubling cells in the bramble, in its red-edged autumn leaves.
Some repetition is seemly: a tractor making loops in a river of grain.
The fieldfare, the redwinged thrush.
Under a white sky wind displaces dust and phosphates.
We even considered: first the yellow willow, then grain, then
the ochre river.
We have held onto seasons and seasons and seasons.

At bus stops rain battered the country new to me.
Grain ripening and rain coming over an ochre river.
I still find holy a field, a tractor looping in it.
In the distance the sound of the train and beyond that the highway.
Some repetition is seemly: as bramble propagates itself and, even so, wild
roses reappear in hedgerows.
The ordinary work of cooking, commuting, thinking, walking.
Under sleeping bags, on layers of cardboard, in alleyways, in train stations.
Wanted the poem to be a kind of singing.
Wanted the poem to be rain on a field and a tractor looping and looping.
Wanted the poem to be redoubling cells in the body of the redwinged
thrush, the fieldfare.
Wanted the poem to run off the fields, along rail lines, in orchards.

With bramble, fieldfare, frost-edged hazel hedgerow, with
ochre river, with sleeping bags, with the hole in the
fencing, with the ordinary work of cooking and walking,
or cells redoubling, or filmstrip finally unlooping.

MINUSCULE SEQUENCE

morning, autumn's
second month
bright blue, half a moon

fresh bitter smell of tea:
red cup, full
my hands, cold

inside my dark dress—
festival!
(orange silk)

grey over yellow
means a storm;
cat takes off down the road

from under the floorboards
a brown spider:
welcome home, uncle

last white geese
making their spare noise,
winter soon

ATTUNEMENT

after Thomas A. Clark

gold arrow
goldfinch

world of ideas
world of things

walking to ocean
the smell of ocean

drinking water
near the sea
smells sea
watery

impossible to leave
the world in
the world

in the museum
that porcelain
cup holding
only its own
shadow

exact shape
of a hand's
negative

morning
all interior
like a Korean cup
a porcelain cup
from the 9th century

the world
the museum
around the cup

goldenrod
golden
goldendrop
ochre

walk through
cut grass
not
a walk
through cut clover

estuary
light

mountain
light

low angle
of light
at sea level

a field
of chicory blue
as fields
of flax
are blue

such two
dissimilar
blues

marginal
weeds find
a way

weedways
where
waterways
were

across wild carrot
lace across goldenrod
shadow
of a raven
is a raven's
call crossing

a museum
a world
in memory
in hand

rivertrout
seatruth
rivertrust
seatrout

the gray-white morning
a grey-white afternoon

comparison
metaphor
similitude
insufficient to
the irreducible
world

humidity
as haze
haze
by humidity

the back cove
lifting
out of the cove

ocean air damply
opening air
oceanic
in apartments
by oceans

under
yarrow all
whitening
continuing

drag
the recycling bin
to the curb
startle
goldfinches

wild riches
of the daily
world
the daily riches
of the wild
world

word world
world word

POINTILISMS

in the footsteps of Sei Shōnagon,
for Neele and Laressa

A little relief when the weather report says, *tomorrow will be warmer than today*, although in the long term it's no relief at all. I look at houses online and estimate how many fruit trees per quarter-acre front garden we could plant.

A small porcelain vase, glazed dark blue, that my friend sent me for my birthday: in the spring it holds a single snowdrop or stem of grape hyacinth. In the winter, a stalk of grass, pale seedhead dry as a whisper.

A snail on the rough surface of the sidewalk: putting out one eye-stalk, then another. Your body moves exactly as it should across the wet ground. Yellow spiral of your shell.

All night, all day: the rain comes in horizontal waves, then vertical waves. Alone in the house, I can hear the place the downspout is missing.

Almost the end of October: and yet I found a violet in bloom, trapped under landscaping net the landlord put down. I too, violet, am caught under the landlord's mesh.

Although I try to look at the world, when I sit down to write, every time, I wish I had paid better attention. Hazelnuts, walnuts, falling in tall grass by the river. Black walnuts dyeing the pavement: if only I had kept the garden where I was unhappy, I would have walnuts to dye some cloth. A little unhappiness—what is that worth?

Autumn woods: the trees along the path begin to thin and blacken; the path itself is covered in bright litter now. Coke can, Gatorade bottle, packet of Cheetos, wrapper of a stick of cherry candy.

Before writing I clear my desk, and I clear my desk again: I can clear my desk for hours before I ever sit to write.

Black branches of the future: you are not, yet. And orange berries of the whitebeam which will shine against its silvery leaves.

Bluetits on the new feeder, wings going so fast they are a blur until they pose on the hanging net of suet and seed. A robin on the feeder.

Cicada song so loud I have to cover my ears sometimes, and it persists from August through October.
A hot-air balloon, blue and orange, rises from a field as if the cicadas lift it.

Even the willows are still mostly in leaf, this late in the season. The mildness persisted so long, and the farmers' market reaps the short-term rewards.

Feedcorn in the road, on the sidewalk, in the gravel driveway; corn chaff in the air: the grain elevator is running again.

I cut a piece from a grapevine covering an entire fence, early September morning, blue sky, water from the air condensing on the translucent wax-green of the leaves. One tendril curling. The green pale grapes like something carved of stone in a museum, but in fact *there*, in front of me, actual grapes.

In the morning, though it isn't that cold, the steam coming from the vent at the side of the building stands out white against the bright brick and the dull dark sky.

It must be that using metaphor is a kind of seeing that permits double vision and extends it. Roadside bush clover, beloved of bees, covered in tiny white flowers—is exactly what it is.

Mars sets through mist in the west, above the Hy-Vee. Let's look at the future, the little red planet says, and it winks and goes out. Meanwhile, my students tell me they will not walk alone in town for fear of interstate kidnaping gangs. I take my bicycle out of the garage, ride loops in the feedlot and over behind the Wal*Mart where Dumpsters perfume the air.

Moonless night, full of rain and the sound of rain, sheeting rain where the gutter overflows above the window, passing trucks lifting water like flanges from the street.

On the dusty asphalt path, a black cat approaches me by zigs and zags, until she can touch my outstretched hand with her cold nose, and then she walks on.

One good thing about cold nights and no heat in the house: the fruit flies mostly die off. In the centre courtyard the abandoned kittens who have made their home in a window well are crying so pitifully. Then one day they are gone, and from my bicycle en route to work I see one smashed on the road.

Pines darkening, where they have not died; some dropped piles of golden needles. One in the group has withered in the lasting drought and heat. Looking up from under these pines into the cloudless sky, I see a red-and-white plastic bag caught in the high branches, flying like a flag.

Some distance between unlike things will recall a grain of similarity.

The branching of the grapevine: how it goes from here, to here, to here, and yet is all one thing.

The feeling of the window closing—the window of the year, the window of youth; and yet I *am* young, and there are many days left in the year. But by seven p.m. it is totally dark outside. White guys in massive pickup trucks drive along our street from Wal*Mart, the engines loud against the night.

The grain elevator runs from early morning until evening. The sun is only up around eight a.m. but the workers arrive when it is still dark, in their fluorescent uniforms.

The grasses behind the hinge-knot fence are heavy with seed, the seeds cluster along each stem like grains of lead on a fishing line. When the wind comes the grasses move, and they all move in the same direction.

The internet plays Debussy on repeat for me, and it is almost as if there is someone here. Almost like company.

The *something* of the world and the *something* of my mind, which is just another word for world, or one of the worlds.

There are six motorcyclists tearing up the road. In a moment they have passed the house, screeching—really, grown men, screeching—as they gun their engines. I don't want to include them in my thinking about the world, but there they are.

Walking in the rain, I realize the sparrows stay hidden when I pass the bushes where they are sheltering, so it may seem to any car driving past that it is only me and my yellow umbrella, under the yellow leaves of black walnuts, ash.

When I get home I put the cut grapevine in the little blue vase my friend sent me, and then I take a photograph and send it to her in our chat. And later I think about the vase and the cutting, and about the students I am trying to reach in our poetry class, and about simile, and I realize how little I know about how the world I think is there works.

When the rain is at its heaviest, my umbrella can barely keep it out; even so, I stop to take a photo of the red leaves against the near-black pavement. Looking at it later, I realize my grey shoes and blue tights, the red leaves, the asphalt, are a beautiful combination of colours.

Where the town sprayed the weeds they were already brown and dry, late autumn before the end of summer, even: the dock stood dark against white stems of grass, as if it were a version in miniature of the roadwork signs stacked against the stockpile of telephone poles in the town's maintenance depot.

You don't get to know, she wrote in her letter, what it will be like to leave until you leave. And you can't know what it was like to be there unless you were there. In any case, it's your life. She wrote that again, and she underlined it. Your life.

OUR ENGLAND

for Jonathan and Neele

This island (not our
island) allowing us
to sit in the sun at a wide
window, with tea—

Where this morning we drove
through hills;
the green of the hills,
the bright
green of them.

(Weak sun even now in April. *How can we know when the thing is finished?* We start pulling bindweed off the old shed, we pull ivy off, we pull buddleia out. The corner of my eye locates a patch of snowdrops, a surprise this late in spring.)

Above in the rowan
a blackbird rasping,
zinging and knocking
like, you said—and you
were being funny,
borrowing language
from this place—you said
'I know not what'
—like *blackbird*:
nothing else like
blackbird.

In quiet you record the pinnate leaf
by moving a needle
by hand over and over
through two layers
of cotton cloth.

'Come to my house
and sing' you say.
We talk about
our future imagined
gardens. A pot of geranium
by the window waves
one red flower
against the pane.

The calls of bluetits and
someone next door playing
the guitar as you sew and I look
at things on the internet.

The man in the dormitory window
and I always wave to one another

when I walk up the hill,
a complaint in my inarticulate calves.

Maple trees beginning to loosen
are the color of nothing
but themselves
a chartreuse brighter than Chartreuse

tipped where they emerge
with brown
and vermilion.

The man with the blue
turban walks by,
meaning: *it is 8:30 a.m.*

At the bus
stop the smell of fresh
air dampening the
wooden bench
its four worn slats.

What is the word for this
sound, rain against glass
in long spatters?

Today along the road a patch
of clover with extremely
large
leaves.

Green uniforms
of ambulance
drivers;
RETURNS cart
in the library also dark
green,

the way dense vegetation is
green from a distance—
a green you cannot see
through.

Craving water
coleus plants
turn pale
pink.

Today the sun
is a white spot
on cloud cover.

We of this time
are not the same

Outside the rain
begins again.

You read to me
I read to you —
We make one another real
in the small warm room
of our foreignness.

Water in the gutter
and along the gutter
snow
or petals.

Today new patterns
of white, black,
green,
bright green, almost
yellow, white:
I cannot determine
all there is
to know
(the snowfall
of wild carrot flower).

A closed-in feeling behind glass.
Above us clouds breaking—
assertion of the verb 'to change'.

Apple, morello cherry, false cherry, crabapple, ornamental pear, grey willow, sea buckthorn; bird cherry, sweet chestnut, hornbeam, wych elm, hazel, alder, wild plum, sloe; ash, oak, yew and lime; muscaria, narcissus with a flat red rill around a yellow face, laburnum, broom. Imported maple. Exuberant rose.

No garden no hedgerow.
'Just a long lovely field of bobolinks,'
the line from the long
poem ringing long
after you read it.

Through all this, air
yellow, verging on green.

By waterways the smell of wet begins.
By daffodils.
By narrowboats, by Sainsbury's,
by cottages (*Grade 2 Listed*), still standing
near the lock.

In living-rooms the smell of damp comes up.
In terraced houses converted to flats.
In between walls, in corridors,
in caravans, the rise of damp goes
on all night.

ABOUT A MONTH

A bulb tossed months ago
in an empty bed
has two bright narrow leaves

Around her table
(red candles, thin china)
us all in one room again

At the old hospital
the dry, tall grass—
here, with tea, with you

Blue descending
everywhere—winter a room
we all live in, darkly

Discarded orchid
on grey pavement;
a grate with iron flowers

Even boiling water
smells good
this morning

Fog in the early hours
then low sun, pink,
on the next-door fields

Four candles,
eight counting their reflections—
a long drive in the dark

Guinea pigs snuffling
in new hay
animal sweetness

Heiße maronen, he calls
and evening touches us
with light fingers

How good and cool
water tastes, waking
too warm at night

In low yellow fields
two horses revel
in new-laid hay

In windows—
perfect circles
perfect eight-pointed stars

Kijk altijd naar wat
onzichtbaar is,
these words, this pink twilight

Last summer's fruit
in my friend's hands:
in my memory, in her kitchen

My finger traces
an architect's name
cut in granite: *I was here*

Name of a flower
for cold months, hellebore—
memory's colour

Neighbours move
in our walls like mice
move in stored grain

No frost yet on the fields—
put in the garlic starts, bring
wood for a fire

Primrose: mistaken,
too early, yellow
as sunrise in winter

Rain at night
and the courtyard full of bicycles:
one window's lit

Roof and magpie
and sharp sky—my mouth
full of liquorice

Screen door built
last summer: whorls
of frost on it now

Shake the apple tree,
an earwig, a spider fall out
(the mice are all asleep)

Smell of pine
through the house:
scent of sap spreads like light

Stark light, last leaf;
sycamore seedheads
vibrate against blue

Swans fly the Leie:
unfrozen, clear and cold
it doubles them

Tea steaming
in the still-cold house
(morning)

Thin branch:
yellow leaves
three golden coins

This dark full
of only December
and strands of light

This time last year:
then too I sat at the desk,
my hands inky

White hyacinth
in a tin can; tea
in our oldest mug

Wind down the chimney—
and poplars leafless,
sycamores leafless

ELEGIES

with hands that wrote you little notes
I write you little elegies

(Millay)

POSTCARD TO SHANA WITH DRAWING OF BLACKBIRDS

It took me *this long* to realize that when the poet
said blackbirds, he meant *blackbirds*: pointing

to the world. (That's just an image in a poem,
though.) Outside, in our now of April rain, two

blackbirds are pulling worms through the lawn's
thatch. It's spring, and soon no one will have

to resemble anyone except their younger self,
who ran out of university buildings in rain

like this, the fine rain of early spring, to steal
daffodils from the sleeping grounds. Write

back to me: my feet are soaking in the sodden grass.
My hands are raw from cold and wet. The table's

set. The light goes through green glass. A jar
of bluebells. Rain glazes grapevine on the panes.

Every warm thing from our girlhood calls us here.
Blackbirds. Poems. The world: its tablecloths

and rainy mornings, cities, hands, and flowers.
Its universities. Its sense of always coming to an end.

Every night in the prairie city, bus drivers play 'Kind of Blue' through boombox speakers on the public bus. I have a CD Walkman now, tape player left behind with childhood. I stand in a wide-open window six stories up from a vacant lot in the middle of the city to watch a band my boyfriend loves, and when they play the only song I like, he kisses me. The patterns imprint themselves: for a long time, this is all I can imagine imagining.

Once when I was very small, my parents took me to a movie theatre. I fell asleep. When I woke up the movie was over and my parents were on either side of me, very quiet, as if the giant room had been built for me to fall asleep on those red velour seats. It was dark. The screen was showing a still image of the outside of the theatre. And we could hear the sound of rain on the roof.

November, month of rain turning to sleet, sleet turning to ice, ice turning to snow, snow piling in drifts around the doors of our apartment buildings, people coming and going from our apartment buildings tracking slush in and warmth out, the sky compressing the city under a shield of lead. In the distance the blue-and-white airplanes take off, their starboard and port lights decorating the air, and before they enter the clouds the passengers at window seats can see the river, only half frozen, light and dark, tracing its oxbows in the land, the stripped trees along it blurring over the snow.

Twelve stories up, in apartment buildings constructed at the utopian peak of the early 1970s, lit windows are just about the same as stars. By winter daylight the red, blue, yellow, white panels that alternate with windows flash where sun hits them. Now, February, night, I pass through concrete courtyards, between columns, where spherical streetlights illuminate paths between garden beds covered in snow. In the elevator it is silent: then the hallway opens in front of me, and I can hear the party down the hall. Knock, open, and *you* are there in the overwhelming room. Out the window twin bridges swing over the Mississippi.

The tiny plane approaches Fargo and the sky seems to go from one side of the world to the other, covering everything, covering *everything*, the snow as bright with stars as the night is, as though someone had spilled light over it. And below, somewhere on the border marked by the Red River, you are waiting, looking up into the sky where two bright dots, one red and one green, are getting closer and closer.

The room I sleep in is almost as cold as outside and ice builds up on the window, causing the wooden rail and stool to rot, just slightly, every winter, until years from now, when I have been living away from home for a decade, the windows will need to be replaced, and the splintery walnut-stained frames of my childhood will give way to new ones that rise easily in their channels. But now it is still 1996, January, and the kitchen is warm because my father has turned the oven on and gone outside to shovel the night's snow in the darkness, shovel giving way to the snowblower only after the neighbours are awake, his hands in big gloves and his green coat bending at the waist as he lifts shovelsful of snow from the sidewalk, and the snow still coming down. My mother and brothers are sleeping and I sit in the kitchen to read the paper before anyone else is there, and the dog, who has now been dead more than half my life, comes to me and puts his head gently on my knee.

Under the bridge two women stand in midair and we walk under their feet every day without marvelling because, after all, it is simply what they do. They stand there, holding up the bridge, their feet gradually wrapped by wild roses, which tangle along that part of the riverbank and bloom magenta for most of July. Then the riverbank is overtaken by goldenrod, and we forget that winter is even a possibility. But the ones who sleep at the feet of the caryatids know that winter is never far away.

Heading west into North Dakota we would drive onto tiny roads dead-ending in corn fields where there was nothing left but stubble and snow, and you would park the car so I could lift up your shirt and unzip your jeans, the cold outside turning our breath to ice on the windows. Wind would come over the empty fields and the icy pellets of snow at 0°F would tick at the car and later we would walk in through the back door at your parents' house, our hair brushed and our college hoodies adjusted, tidy, careful, clean, secretive, completely in love, entirely certain that we were the only grown-ups in the room.

At the Halloween party my friends kissed boys in the dark corners of an eighth-grade basement while I sat in the well-lit kitchen upstairs and talked to their parents. Sara came to school the next day listening to Nirvana. Did I know this music, she asked, but no, I didn't. I usually put my dad's copy of 'Revolver' on the turntable at home. The radio tuned itself automatically to KBEM-FM, The Twin Cities' Only Jazz Station. When Sara showed up in class a while later crying because Kurt Cobain had killed himself I had to reveal I didn't know what suicide was, either. Through the window in the bathroom where we whispered to one another, I could see a single branch, leafless in every season.

In this cabinet, a collection of rusty metal found near train tracks outside Chicago, some pieces of broken encaustic tile, porcelain, sea glass, a five-inch-tall bottle of medicinal lemonade from the last century, minus stopper. Here is a portable CD player that still works, requiring four double-A batteries. Here is a scrap of paper with an AOL screen name and password in teenage handwriting. Here is a mailbox full of weekly letters, here is a bus transfer (the paper kind, punched by the driver), here is a library card for the Minneapolis Public Library System, here is a t-shirt washed in detergent that smells like being no older than 19 circa 1998. Here is a notebook with poems copied out carefully: you and I walked down the pedestrian street among skyscrapers reciting Dickinson, and above us the crows filled the empty branches of winter oaks.

The gas station closed, the movie store closed, the Perkins closed and there will never again be overnight pancakes to be had that cheap anywhere in town. The elementary school got a bomb threat and sent letters home. The public library reduced its hours. The playground burned down. The Dairy Queen closed down and then reopened. The tattoo parlour, the pizza place swing their front doors wide in the late summer humidity, it's over 80°F even at night and the yellow streetlamps diffuse through air so saturated you can almost see it. Finally the heat breaks and the humidity turns into rain, which we stand in, at three in the morning, because if we stop holding onto one another the world as it is will start turning and we will return to the present, to our grown-up selves, to the facts of cities and betrayals and time passing, the facts of ordinary life.

Northern pike rode through water, their dorsal fins breaching it; bass and bowfin, rainbow trout, yellow perch rising for mayflies at the still surface. We headed out along gravel-paved rural routes where balls of string grew immense in houses that survived the Great Depression. We ran through cornfields we knew could cut us, peered through the glass into greenhouses where botanists touched cuttings with willow rooting solution. And snow came, and mist rose from the river: and the thaw in February sent runners out rejoicing on the public paths in fluorescent orange nylon shorts.

Because I believed that I could always return, I left the beloved city where I had lived since childhood: among Somali women in their flowered dresses crossing its dozen bridges; among the poets falling or flying from the same; among Hmong grandmothers selling bitter melon and spring onions at the farmers' market on Nicollet Mall; among six-plex apartment houses in whose drawers were hidden decks of cards printed with airline companies' names; among affordable Chinese restaurants catering to homesick students from Chengdu and Hong Kong, away from which I carried in those years (on my bicycle, through blizzards) hundreds of white wax-paper boxes. I left behind anonymous notes tied to my handlebars—*I love you. Free Lunch At Armoury Today. Have you seen this cat?* All spring, all my life the mornings were cool and blue, and on autumn afternoons I fell asleep to football on t.v., across the lap of someone I loved. *The future* descended as surely as rain: all day and all night.

How many times I sat in a second-floor cafeteria and longed to see someone I knew, feeling so far from home despite being close to home that I would have taken *anyone*—a school bully, an acquaintance who shared a row in lecture—even without a greeting, even without their having seen me, as a sign that I was not alone. I would track people I recognized as they chose among plastic-wrapped bouquets in the grocery store. Once, from across a bookshop, I saw someone I had met briefly at a party on the twelfth floor of a utopian apartment complex, and raised one hand, and he turned, then, and saw me, and after just a moment's hesitation, raised his hand to me in return, and so I went to him, and walked over bridges with him, and wrote letters to him, and received notes from him, and brought dinner to him, late in the architecture classrooms, building models for the next day's class, and descended to him on the plains that had been carved into the states of Minnesota and North Dakota, between the wings of a tiny aluminium vessel blinking alternately red and green.

Mist rising from the river at seven in the morning on a school day in the depths of winter. It is 1998. I will skip my last period class, take the number 10 bus northbound to sit in the waiting room at a high school in a suburb until the last bell goes, I will touch my boyfriend's skin under his shirt standing at another bus stop for twenty minutes waiting for the number 10 bus southbound to appear, its double lights and its numerical display brightening the afternoon, which falls faster and faster as our part of the planet tilts away from the sun. Later I will be able to compare the speed with which the light changes back in the settler city on the edge of the prairie to the way it changes in England and in Flanders. As a child I learned to sense the depth of snow by looking out the window, and I knew what real cold was. Landing in Europe in a September of the new millennium I had no idea I was about to see: a rose that truly did bloom all through winter.

I got on my blue Schwinn and headed to the architecture studios where you were working late. I stole pieces of arbor vitae for their scent when crushed; I lay on the floor with my head on a rolled-up jacket while thirteen students did CAD drawings after midnight. Outside, among the Brutalist buildings, peonies began to unwrap themselves. Under the tables I could see the names of people who by now had lives and cities of their own: hearts and dates, telephone numbers. The world was static in those days, even when we tried to speed it up, listening to the radio in your car with the windows down, speeding the empty highways of western Minnesota and kissing one another until our mouths were bruised.

Breathe in, breathe out, time passes and flashes and once again we are swinging one another around in the air, jumping up and down to Reel Big Fish and Save Ferris; we're in the caves under the bluffs; we are pumping our pedals to cross the Tenth Avenue Bridge, the Washington Avenue Bridge, the railroad bridge, the bridges downtown in this settler city; we are spinning in the park under the snow which never stops coming down. In wooden houses the parents who love us are worrying about us but we are only sleeping tucked into one another in twin beds. We are only sharing files on Napster and staying up too late. We carry groceries home in our arms. We go to the movies. We are just at the edge of everything, here on the prairies at the end of history. You light up the dark, at the top of the apartment building near the river. I'm flying and flying, over highways, over everything. Ever so lightly, we step across the boundary into spring. The ice goes out. The mist rises once again from the river.

SELF-STUDY

The commitment I made was holding my breath. As I had
learned to speak your language: almost without breathing.

Your hands are just your hands. The lines in your face.
And yet, precious. I never saw you touch anything

so gently as you touched me. —Not true: every
dog, the car you worked on, flowers you brought

in white paper, glass of water you filled, window
as you passed your hand along the curtain. Ocean

at Oostende. Even the pen you used to sign
the documents we had to sign. I cannot see words

in Dutch without seeing them in your voice.
Who finally when I breathed out I left behind.

ALONG THE LEIE, FIELDS FULL OF THE MEMORY

of flax, night turning July to August, a dark
sky's small lights doubled in the river:

under our sleeping windows where the hush of air
is crossing low lands from the ocean, the beautiful
boy comes with his hair shining in the headlights

like actual gold.
                    Nothing but cliché can be spoken
of the dead, who live in their distant cities without
us, who are there whole, untouched and singly

crowned by death. The smallness of the body
surrounded by its corona of broken windshield. All
that remains to say of them is a shrine words anyway

cannot approach—so in their places we plant trees, lay
narrow stones, leave candles flickering in jars, say
novenas, make the sense of missing *something* up

with bears and ribbons, roadside photographs, credible
apparitions, letters, avoidance, small Xes on a map—
of course there *is* something missing,

regardless of belief, and we know it: in the cool
night air which bears the stars dispassionately,
with no thought for our need or lack

of language, the bodies of boys outline themselves
in roadside grasses, where water will pool
in late winter, where red and pink poppies will blow

among cornflowers, wild roses; where the tiny, pale blue star-shaped earthly blossoms of the flax will spell their names, in all the languages beyond the ones we know.

SONNET IN EARLY SPRING

Despite our losses, we still have the sky,
bright blue in April, and the river here—
half-ice, translucent, snow diminished by
the angle of the sun. The trees are spare
and black against that blue.
                                        —I *know* things change,
that pattern is our life. Things come, things pass.
The difference in days is more a hinge
than the black/white departure it can seem it is.

Stopping for death? In fact, the world goes on.
But in its steady shifting it consoles:
the days that pass also return what's gone.
Beneath the thinning ice, the river flows.
Winter recedes. Spring comes. That's all we know:
this world holds us, will not let us go.

POEM FOR YOUR BROTHER

—with a phrase from Brooks

He should have had this day, when it has finally stopped
raining in New Hampshire and things are the *green*
that you can use along the new-paved road
to your parents' house, where apple trees

bloom, and the last cold has gone from the brook running
diagonal and downhill, away. You'd want this for him:
your father's smell after chopping wood, even
ache in your right shin where one log sprang

back from the axe and struck bone. Flight of crows
from high treetops, tin cans disintegrating. You would
want years—

His hair curling, brush-thick, black, who held you
upside-down underwater, chased girls, loved
skateboards, trucks, the odour of his nephews' sleeping
breath, chicory springing summer-skyward

by the roadway, mountain covered
in leafed-in trees. His heart's good, your brother,
who left the television loud so someone would wonder,
call the super, so it wouldn't be your mother finding him.

When the rain comes again
all of you will be under its grey roof; the mornings
will seem fine until you remember and, outside,
an oriole, misplaced, will pull

six thin notes from air, bending branches
orange and black—there is no going back,
despite every *should*: it will fly away.

HISTORY OF THE HIGHWAYS OF THE UNITED STATES

Someone says your names at a distance and they could be the names of our brothers, names of bridges, names of towns now crumbling after years of depopulation, names of the highways themselves: *Been-here-before. Swear-not. Take-no-prisoners.* Coal miners lose their tongues somewhere in Pennsylvania, and the company pays out nothing but the memory of hills that look blue and turn deadly, taste of dust, rust in a cut hand, a wind blowing through left laundry. The asphalt factory closed too. In the green atlas the world changes shape and the roads have been erased one by one, the pink nub moving back and forth on one page until it goes through to the next. Now what seemed to be a country looks like the edge of rocks, sixty-foot drop to grey-blue quarry water, where boys swing out on old rope. Smell of moss decomposing a set of wooden stairs. A chain of electrified cars came through the Adirondacks earlier this year carrying nothing but the familiar sound of death. Fill up jars with grave dirt in Oklahoma. Ship oranges and their parasites from California across the Great Plains. The fens of the central territories were drained for military conquest and the railroad and became Iowa, on which a hundred Wal*Marts were erected. Under the low spine of the Turtle Mountains a second row of teeth breaks our national gums. We're still listening for a sign of our brother coming home late.

SONNET FOR OCTOBER TO MARCH

The garden's autumn, daily, is an end:
the heavy heads of sunflowers all are bent
toward the ground, and finches come to eat
what seeds remain. Zucchini leaves are white.
I know the way October makes me grieve
has everything to do with other loss.
But when the flocks of starling start to leave,
the days feel like a sober bit of cloth

or ribbon that has had bright threads pulled out.
It takes some time for eyes like mine to see
that starkness doesn't end the world's thought;
that dark and quiet days may signify
a common miracle: life after death—
advancing spring. The *out*
                                        and *in* of breath.

FAMILY MATH

Some Sundays we went to the house on the hill
where for years our grandmother boiled tea and served it

black with Vienna Fingers we dunked. The kettle
was aluminium and we thought that was what made her sick

so then our mother went to take care of her every day.
When we visited, our refined, Irish grandmother

threw a bowl of soggy shredded wheat.
No more kettles screeching to a stop on the green stove.

Linen towels bundled around packets of mail.
Our aunts' clown doll face-down in the closet. Boxes

of unopened cereal, last year's swim cap, a trail
of talcum powder through the house. We watched

from the stair rail, poking our heads in between for photos.
The people we loved receded into the distance:

we didn't understand what *zero* meant, but did our math
at the kitchen table while storms came in across the street.

HEMISPHERIC SHIFT

Sandpipers blown off course
and far from ocean.
The earliest hurricane recorded

a month earlier than ever, three
months earlier, until fire
season, hurricane season happen

all year. In December the tornado
sirens go off, and then
in March. But you know all

about this. You told me the brain
has a second home
in the intestines, you said

nothing doesn't touch
the rest of everything. You
taught yourself to walk, write,

look, not fall, think, keep
track, take care. Again.
We said you were lucky

and we meant we were,
but at Christmas you told us
it would have been easier to die.

You did not die.
You insisted everyone
stay alive with you.

You pulled up the lawn
and put in flowers.
I pretended not to notice

the frogs with five legs. Six legs.
The mercury rose in November.
Underwater, midges began

to wake up. Blood had
come from a tiny hole
in your brain's membrane.

We walk your neighbourhood
watching for fascist graffiti
and monarchs on milkweed.

Before your stroke, we
counted on distinctions: *this*
is summer, *that* is where

migratory birds occur. This place,
that place. Between the brain's two halves,
you said, now any impossible thing can happen.

WAKE

With Dickinson, acrostic

In the room was his breathing, and we were, and
this day of days was, the quality of *lastingness* hiding how
short such long moments are. We waited. Our
life continued, endlessly, all afternoon, as the breath
that was the sound of his dying underwrote the house.
Only breath, and us, and the October sun, and *nothing*
lasts, despite eternity's illusion, despite how long a day,
an hour feels, despite the ordinary reliability of breath, and
hours, and days, and fathers, and Octobers. An end.

How long we waited, on the bed's chenille cover, then; how
much music we played for him on our phones, on the guitar,
how we sang, in those last hours, prayed, read poems, how
little any bitterness mattered, then. How the youngest lay
his head on our father's translucent shoulder, then. Nothing
within the circle broken. The day a golden-blue October day.
Our bringing of water, our sponging of his mouth, our small
powers. His breath that was and was and was, and then:

AN AMPLER – ZERO –

'for some – an Ampler Zero – '
(Emily Dickinson)

—Scilla appear over snow's diminishing. The upright narrow leaves and blue-turning-white-turning-purple buds of scilla, opening as the sun returns to its equinoctial habits. The *nothing* of the snow's going supplanted by the everything of *here* the flowers say.

—'The body will be reduced to ash.' *To reduce*, she says, meant *to bring back* before it ever came to mean *to diminish*. She is holding the dictionary open, telling me she doesn't know enough yet to begin the thing she wants to write.

—What if you weren't *waiting* (as if sitting at the end of a long corridor, hearing the voices of the others faintly from behind a door and waiting your turn to be called in: *I'm ready!*) but already, even as you sat there in the hallway's pale fluorescence, *in the midst* of something (your life)?

—The adventitious bulbs of scilla spread; the seeds flung by dying flowers last spring germinate in the damp earth, which absorbs the last of the snow. Soon the apple trees will open pinkening arms, blossoms fill the branches so that spring resembles orchards full of snow.

—Oh hang on, she says. It also means *to bring to a different state*, and later *to a simpler or lower state.* When she puts the dictionary down on the feather pillow it sounds like nothing being set on top of nothing.

—What if, sitting in the winter hallway, as strangers pass and the sound of a drip somewhere in the pipes echoes and echoes, your life were *coming toward you*: what if your life were not winter receding but spring returning, an advancing tapestry of tiny blue flowers close to the earth, and, caught on each, the myriad baubles of the melting snow; among which flowers, lying down, you yourself might be brought back to

—a wider kind of *nothing* in which *nothing* disappears but is transformed; the ampler *zero* of the infinitesimal movements of flowers against the melting of the snow; a waiting room where the dead are always with us—

—springtime, the Milky Way, pearl-coloured antechamber, waning and waxing garden, corona and corolla, alpha and omega, a forever of spring after the forever of winter, amplitude of ordinary breath, infinity of zeroes?

ACKNOWLEDGEMENTS

Grateful acknowledgment is made to the editors of the magazines where some of these poems first appeared, often in very different versions:

'Sonnet for ordinary time', *Beloit Poetry Journal*
'Sonnet for the second-language speaker', *Poetry Ireland Review*
'February mother', *Poetry Ireland Review*
'*Broken Blue and White Handled Mug*, Maker Unidentified' won an *ARTWORD* prize from the Maine Writers & Publishers Alliance and the Portland (ME) Museum of Art, 2021
'Postcard to Shana with photograph of Floraliën Ghent, 1913', *PN Review*
'A note on early Flemish painting', *Beloit Poetry Journal*
'Waterway connecting the city to the sea: image and commentary', *PN Review*
'Signification', *PN Review*
'Corona borealis' in *Heavenly Bodies*, Beautiful Dragons, 2014
'About a month', as 'December' in *Off the Beaten Track: a Year in Haiku*, Boatwhistle Books, 2016
'Postcard to Shana with drawing of blackbirds', *PN Review*
'Along the Leie, fields full of the memory', *Maine Sunday Telegram*
'Wake', *Poetry Ireland Review*

Grateful acknowledgment is also made to Dancing Girl Press, publisher of the chapbook *Sweetbriar*, where some of these poems appeared in earlier forms.

* * *

In the poem 'About a month', the German phrase just means 'hot chestnuts' and the Dutch phrase means 'always look at what is unseeable'

* * *

The following borrowings/quotations occur across the book:

The epigraph to the collection is used by kind permission of Dr. Gareth Farmer and the Estate of Veronica Forrest-Thomson. 'Postcard to Shana with photo of Washington Avenue Bridge (Minneapolis)' makes reference to the poet John Berryman, who died jumping from that bridge in 1972; the bridge crosses the Mississippi and links two parts of the University of Minnesota campus. 'Vocational Education' quotes part six of *Leaves of Grass*, which calls the grass 'the handkerchief of the Lord / A scented gift and remembrancer designedly dropt' and also makes reference to an anecdote about Richard Hugo walking out of a classroom through a window, which I was told as a student by my teacher. 'Desiderata' uses a quotation from Dickinson's poem 1755 ('To make a prairie') as an epigraph. 'Sonnet with a quotation from Millay' begins with the first line from a sonnet ('V' from *Renascence and Other Poems*, 1917) by Edna St Vincent Millay. 'Our England' contains a line from the poem 'Flare' by Mary Oliver—'just a long lovely field of bobolinks'. 'Postcard to Shana with picture of blackbirds' makes reference to Wallace Stevens' poem 'Thirteen Ways of Looking at a Blackbird'. 'Everything solid melts into air' is not my phrase but belongs to the translators of Karl Marx. 'Poem for your brother' contains part of a line from the Gwendolyn Brooks poem 'To The Young Who Want To Die'. 'Sonnet in early spring' makes oblique reference to Dickinson's poem 479 ('Because I could not stop for Death –'). 'Wake' uses the entirety of Dickinson's poem 1292 ('In this short Life that only lasts an hour / How much – how little – is within our power'), adapted, as an acrostic. 'An ampler—zero—' takes its title from Dickinson's poem 422 ('More Life – went out – when He went').

* * *

Thanks to Jon McGregor, Matthew Welton, Carol Rowntree Jones, Pippa Hennessy, and Neele Dellschaft, who were my companions in writing and thinking during the early drafting of many of these poems. To Sue Peng Ng, Sriparna Ray, Jonathan Vanhaelst and the literary and living beings of Nottinghamshire, also companions during those years. Thanks to the many people on either side of the Leie to whom I belonged for some of my time writing these as well. 'Along the Leie...' is for the Vanhaelst/Van Rechem family. (The Leie is a river in Flanders.) 'Poem for your brother' is for the Aldrich family.

There are many poets and poems woven through this book, a testimony to my teachers—especially Miss Evanson who taught us to make books in sixth grade and let me copy poems into mine, and professors Michael Dennis Browne and Ray González, who shaped my understanding of poetry as something shared, open, exultant, and to be carried around in my body. This book is also a testimony to the poet-friends of my young adulthood, especially Zachary, with whom I learned to do what our teachers told us: exult, make poems, carry them around.

Finally, this book was possible because my parents, despite difficulties, made a house where books, music, pictures, and imagining were central to our lives and because, as William Stafford wrote, "Little folded paws, judge me: I came away", and have looked back ever since across the distance of migration and adulthood. These poems are for the people who were in the room—my mother Líadán, Nuala, Grania, Michael, Kristyn, Cullen, Amy, Gus, Noah, Randa, and Matt. And, in the end and at the beginning, this book is for Shana, who showed up out of nowhere in 2002, quoted Millay in response to my own quotations, and has accompanied me in the shared field of poetry ever since.